April '09

To Mark,

Kristie C. Jones
& Mia

Stories From Black Dog Ranch

Dog Tales About Hope and Second Chances

Written by Kristie C. Jones
Illustrated by Gena E. Faulkner

Stories From Black Dog Ranch:
Dog Tales About Hope and Second Chances
ISBN: 978-0-9817830-0-0
Copyright© by Kristie C. Jones
Illustrated by Gena E. Faulkner

This book is based on true stories.
All rights reserved. No parts of the material protected by this copyright notice may be reproduced or used in any form or by any means, electronic or mechanical, including photocopying, recording, or by any information storage and retrieval system, without prior written permission of the copyright owner.

Printed in the United States
Design and layout
by BRIO, Minneapolis, Minnesota

Contact information:
Black Dog Ranch Publications
P.O. Box 412
Farmington, MO 63640
or visit our website at
www.blackdogrescueranch.com

Introduction

Hi, my name is Mia. I have lots of brothers and sisters and we all live with Ms. Charlene at Black Dog Ranch.

Most of us are not true brothers and sisters, but we are a real family just the same. Ms. Charlene says what makes our family so special is a whole lot of variety.

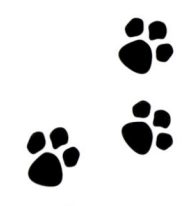

Some of us are short and some are tall. Some have tails and some have no tails. Some of us are lean and some are a little plump. Some of us have ears that stand up and some have ears that are floppy. We even have a few horses living here at the ranch. I guess the reason Ms. Charlene named our farm the Black Dog Ranch is because most of us are black dogs and she said it just seemed fitting to name our farm the Black Dog Ranch. I have lots of stories about how we all came to live here so pull up a chair on the front porch and I'll get started.

Mia, Mickey and Molly's Story

It's still a little scary to think back to that cold winter night long ago when Mickey, Molly and I ended up on Ms. Charlene's front porch.

We lived with our dog Mother on an old pig farm down the road. The night we were born Mother said she remembered hearing the pig farmer telling his wife that they couldn't afford to feed anymore dogs and that he was going to take us to the dump and just leave us there to make it on our own somehow.

Well from that moment on Mother started looking for a place to take us, a place where we would be safe and cared for, a place far away from that old pig farmer.

Mother would hide us in the hay shed at night and then go out looking for a good place for us to live. One night when we were hiding in the shed Mother came back right away. She said that she had been

watching Ms. Charlene's place and had even gone up there. She told us Ms. Charlene leaves lots of food out on her front porch and never chases away any stray dog wanting something to eat. Mother said she believed with all of her heart that Ms. Charlene would take us in and take good care of us even though

she already had several strays living there on her farm.

So that very night we waited until all the lights in the pig farmer's house went out and we started off on our journey to Ms. Charlene's.

It was very cold that night and had started to snow. We were still very small puppies and Mother worried about us making the trip, but she knew it was our only hope so she kept pushing us on.

It seemed like it took nearly all night for us to cross the meadows and forest that lay between the pig farm and Ms. Charlene's. We had never traveled so far before and I kept telling Mother we couldn't go on much longer but finally we had made it all the way to Ms. Charlene's front porch.

The other dogs that were living there had come out to see what was going on. Mother went over and talked to them for a while and then she came back to where she had left us. She told us all stray dogs have kind of an understanding with each about needing a home and someone to care for them so they walked back to where they had been sleeping and left us there with our Mother to say our goodbyes.

    Mother told us how much she loved us and that even though we couldn't be together any longer her love would always be with us. Her job was watching over the pig farm and she couldn't stay at Ms. Charlene's.

    She told me that it would be up to me to watch after my brother and sister and she would be depending on me to take over from now on. I was so frightened; I mean I was just a puppy myself. Although I was very sad about never seeing my Mother again I told her I would be brave and do my best.

    Mother left us that night on Ms. Charlene's front porch with a heavy heart, but full of hope that there would be a future and a better life

for me and my brother and sister.

After we watched our beloved Mother walk off into the darkness we found a big pile of leaves at the far side of the front porch and that is where we huddled together to wait for what we didn't know. Eventually Mickey and Molly fell fast asleep.

Very early the next morning we were suddenly awakened by a loud bang. It was the front door to Ms.

Charlene's house. I looked up and saw her standing there. She had a funny looking hat on her head, a big fuzzy sweater wrapped around herself and two little dogs with ropes attached to their collars.

Those little dogs were hopping and jumping around at the end of those ropes and seemed to be so happy to be outside on such a cold morning. We were trying to be as quiet as we could be because we didn't know what was going to happen when Ms. Charlene discovered us there on her porch.

Well it didn't take long for those two little dogs to sniff us out. They ran right up to us and began jumping all over us. We were so scared we couldn't move then suddenly I felt my brother and sister crawl behind me. There I was face to face with Ms. Charlene. She was just standing there looking down at me.

I was trying hard to remember what Mother had told me about being brave, but when Mickey and Molly started to whimper I felt my legs and ears tremble.

Ms. Charlene slowly bent down and held her hand out to me. I still remember how she spoke to me for the first time that morning. There was so much tenderness in her voice. I could see in her eyes all the warmth and love that my Mother had assured us we would find at Ms. Charlene's. She reached over and gently patted me on the head. I knew from that moment on that life was

going to be great for Mickey, Molly and me.

    Ms. Charlene spent the rest of that day making a new place for us to live. She put up a little picket fence and right in the middle of it she put a big doghouse with lots of blankets in it.

    She gave us food to eat and clean water to drink. She even gave us toys and chew bones to play with. We had never seen such things, why we never had a single toy when we lived on that pig farm. It was going to be everything our Mother had hoped for us at Ms. Charlene's.

Teddie's Story

I guess you could say Teddie is the leader of our pack here at Black Dog Ranch. He watches out for us making sure we stay away from any dangers that might be lurking in the woods behind our farm. He likes to

sit on the front porch so he can keep an eye on everything that goes on around here. Teddie didn't have a very happy life before he came to live here at the ranch. I still remember the first day I met Teddie.

It had been raining hard most of the day and we were snuggled together sleeping in our doghouses.

Late that afternoon we woke to the sound of a rusty old truck speeding up the road in front of the ranch. A young girl was hanging her head out of the window calling for Ms. Charlene. She turned into the driveway and skidded to a stop. She was still yelling for Ms. Charlene as she jumped out of the truck and pulled Teddie out of the back seat.

Ms. Charlene had just opened the front door of the house when

the girl ran up to her dragging poor Teddie along behind.

Me and the others had gathered around the front porch to get a better look at this new dog when I heard the girl telling Ms. Charlene that her uncle had decided he no longer wanted this dog and was going to do something bad to him.

    She told Ms. Charlene she had heard of our farm and that it might be a place to take an unwanted dog She was pleading with Ms. Charlene to help Teddie. She said it was his only hope of escaping the cruel fate her uncle had decided for him.

    I remember looking into Teddie's eyes that afternoon. There was so much sadness in them. You could tell that it hadn't been easy for him. He was unwanted. I could see that he had never been shown any love or kindness as he stood there with his head down. He had lost all hope of anything good in his life long ago.

    I looked up at Ms. Charlene and I saw that she too could see how sad Teddie was. When the girl finished her story I heard Ms. Charlene tell her that we would be honored for Teddie to live here with us at Black Dog Ranch. She said as long as she was able that she would never turn away an unwanted dog that needed a loving home.

    So that summer afternoon began Teddie's life of devotion to Ms. Charlene. I don't think I have ever seen another dog love Ms. Charlene the way Teddie does. Oh we all love

Ms. Chalene, but Teddie never leaves her side and where she goes he is sure to follow.

Ms. Charlene told Teddie that afternoon that he was beautiful and special and she would always love him and care for him. Since that day he came to live at Black Dog Ranch he knows what it means to be loved and wanted.

He has his freedom here at the ranch. The chains that held him down for so long are gone.

Ms. Charlene has a very special place in her heart for Teddie and I guess we all do.

Wila and Betty's Story

Wila and Betty were some of the first pups to live at Black Dog Ranch. Wila told me all about it a few months after my brother, sister and I came to live at the ranch.

Wila has always been uneasy around strangers. She doesn't trust just anyone unless Ms. Charlene tells her they are okay. She told me the reason is because of the way her and Betty were taken away from their Mother and abandon as young puppies.

Wila and Betty were born in an old run down apartment building at the edge of town. Their Mother had belonged to the landlord of those apartments and he had kept her around to keep an eye on things when he wasn't there.

    Wila said that the landlord wasn't very happy the night he found out about her Mother having puppies and after that night her Mother worried about what he might do to Wila and Betty.

Well a few months had passed and everything seemed to be fine when one day the landlord showed up again. He tied their Mother to a fence so she couldn't follow after him and with Wila and Betty in the back of his truck he headed out of town.

He drove them to a creek way out in the middle of nowhere and took them out of the truck.

Wila told me she thought the landlord was just stopping to let them play in the creek when the next thing she knew he was driving away without them.

Wila said that's when she and Betty realized they would never see their Mother again.

After several days of being frightened and hungry and all

alone down at that creek the two of them had given up all hope of being rescued when a real miracle happened......

It was a spring day when Ms. Charlene started out on one of her trips to visit friends across town.

Ms. Darla and she had been close friends for many years. Ms. Charlene and Ms. Darla had a lot in common, they both opened their homes and hearts to unwanted dogs and other animals.

That day when Ms. Charlene arrived Ms. Darla had prepared a nice lunch for the two of them and after catching up on what was new they decided to take a walk around Ms. Darla's farm.

They started out crossing the meadow and then followed a path that lead down to a little creek at the edge of the farm.

They stopped at the creek to watch a little school of fish swimming around in the water when suddenly they heard something moving around in the bushes on the other side. They were trying to be very quiet so they wouldn't frighten whatever was over there when all of a sudden Ms. Charlene saw something that looked like two little black ears popping up out of the bushes.

Ms. Charlene looked at Ms. Darla and at the same time they said, "it's a puppy"! They tried calling to the puppy but it was too scared to come out of the bushes. They knew the only way to get to the puppy was to cross the creek so in they went. It wasn't very deep but the water was chilly so they hopped across quickly.

When they reached the bushes where they had seen the puppy to their surprise two puppies jumped out. Ms. Charlene and Ms. Darla just stood there speechles.

After getting a closer look at the two puppies Ms. Charlene could tell they had not eaten in a few days and they were still very young. She told Ms. Darla that they needed to get the puppies back to the house so they each scooped up a puppy and headed back.

    Once they had fed the puppies and cleaned them up they decided that Ms. Charlene would take them home with her. Ms. Darla had already taken in several strays that spring and at the time Ms. Charlene only had a couple of little house dogs living at her farm.

    Wila said that by the time Ms. Charlene had gotten her and Betty home they were both very sick puppies. She said that Ms. Charlene never gave up on the two of them and after several months of good food and special medicine they both grew into happy healthy dogs.

Now they spend their days playing together and sleeping the afternoons away on Ms. Charlene's front porch.

Wila doesn't trust just any stranger, but she sure is glad she trusted Ms. Charlene that day long ago down by that creek.

Maggie and Charlie's Story

I guess in order for me to tell you the story of how Maggie and Charlie came to live here I'll have to go all the way back to the beginning when Ms. Charlene herself first came to live here at Black Dog Ranch.

Ms. Charlene had spent many years living and working in the big city and she had always said that if she ever had a farm of her own she was going to take in unwanted dogs.

For years she had watched her share of dogs trying to survive on the city streets, but she had no place to keep so many that needed homes.

Ms. Charlene had grown up on a big farm and as a little girl she had

dogs, horses and all sorts of farm animals. She learned from her Father how important it was to take proper care of animals.

She knew then she had a special connection with animals and that someday she would have her own farm where she could care for those animals that no one else wanted.

Well the day finally came when Ms. Charlene finally saved up enough money to buy that little farm. It was way out in the country on an old dusty road.

The old farmhouse wasn't much to look at but it had a big front porch and Ms. Charlene thought with a little time and some tender loving care she could fix it up to be a fine

home and a good place for some of those animals no one else wanted.

Ms. Charlene spent the next several months that spring fixing up the old farmhouse and then she decided she was finally ready to adopt her first puppy.

She started off that afternoon on a trip back to the big city to her old neighborhood. She had heard

from a friend still living there about an old woman who had a small dog with a litter of tiny puppies. The old woman told the friend she couldn't keep them and put them out in the alley with a sign that said "free puppies".

Ms. Charlene knew that small house dogs and their puppies could not survive very long outside without some sort of shelter so she was on her way back to her old neighborhood to bring those puppies and the mother home to the farmhouse.

When Ms. Charlene finally arrived at the house she was surprised to find there was only one little puppy left.

Several nice people passing by

earlier that day had stopped when they saw the box. Two of the puppies along with the Mother had already gone to good homes.

Ms. Charlene said the last little puppy was no bigger that the palm of her hand, but had the biggest ears she had ever seen. She said the puppy was so funny looking that it was down right adorable so she put the puppy in her truck and started back home.

Ms. Charlene said from the very first day she brought Maggie home

with her she was the perfect little house dog.

Several months later, while making one of her weekly trips to town, Ms. Charlene saw another friend that worked for a pet store.

The friend told Ms. Charlene about some puppies that had been brought to them buy a man that raised puppies. She told Ms. Charlene the pet store couldn't sale one of the puppies because he had a crippled leg. The lady told Ms. Charlene they were having a hard time just finding a home for him.

Ms. Charlene told her friend that she would be glad to take the little puppy and it didn't matter to her about the puppy's leg she would give him a good home.

    After picking up her supplies that day Ms. Charlene went back to the pet store to bring her new puppy home.

    Ms. Charlene and Maggie took one look at Charlie and instantly fell in love. Why they never even noticed that he had a crippled leg. Ms. Charlene said Charlie has been one of her biggest blessings. She said when we open our hearts to those with special needs we realize how much love they have to give.

Well that is how Ms. Charlene started the ranch and adopted her very first dogs. Maggie and Charlie spend their days inside the old farmhouse playing together and sleeping their days away. You know none of us have ever noticed Charlie's leg either, we all think he's a pretty handsome little house dog.

Sugar and Gracie's Story

Dogs aren't the only thing being rescued here at Black Dog Ranch. Sugar and Gracie are horses that needed a home and someone to take care of them.

I was sitting on the front porch that afternoon when Ms. Charlene came driving up in the old farm truck pulling a trailer along behind it.

We have learned to expect that every now and then Ms. Charlene is going to show up here at the ranch with another addition to our family. Well that day we couldn't wait to see who she had brought home.

When Sugar and Gracie step out of that trailer it was easy to see why Ms. Charlene ended up bringing them to the ranch.

They were very thin and I could tell right away that they had been terribly neglected so I made it a point to let them know that they had come to the right place and Ms. Charlene would take good care of them....

It was right in the middle of winter that year when Ms. Charlene rescued Sugar and Gracie. She had been passing by this little farm on her way into town when she had noticed two very thin horses standing in an old dirt lot.

Ms. Charlene said that there wasn't any hay for them to eat and she wasn't even sure if they had water to drink.

Day after day as Ms. Charlene would drive past her heart would break for those poor helpless horses.

    Soon after the weather started getting cold Ms. Charlene could take no more so one afternoon she decided to stop.

    She walked up to a raggedy old house trailer sitting at the back of that dirt lot and she knocked on the door. She wasn't even sure if anyone lived there when finally a young man answered.

    Ms. Charlene didn't want to accuse the young man of mistreating his horses so instead she offered him some help. She told him she had been driving by on her way to town and had noticed that his horses were out of hay. She said she had bought extra hay that year and would be happy to let him have as much as he needed.

    The young man was clearly ashamed of the way his horses looked. He told Ms. Charlene that he had lost his job and was having a hard time trying to feed them and his family. He told her that if he could find a home for the horses he would be willing to give them up.

Well I guess you know what Ms. Charlene did. She went back that very day with the trailer and took Sugar and Gracie home with her.

It took nearly all winter for Ms. Charlene to get Sugar and Gracie back to health and looking like the other horses here at the ranch. She spent all of her spare time at the barn giving them lots of feed and hay.

Every morning and every evening we would all follow Ms. Charlene up to the barn and wait for her as she fed them and cared for them.

All of us here at the ranch know that love can heal a broken heart and sometimes It can find a way to bring those that are forgotten home.

    By the next spring Sugar and Gracie were feeling like real horses again. Every afternoon we would sit on the front porch with Ms. Charlene and watch them grazing in the pasture.

    Now every time they see Ms. Charlene outside they will come up to the fence and give her a whinny before running off to play with their friends.

Baby Blaze's Story
(Little Britches)

I guess the story about Baby Blaze is about as sad as things can get for an unwanted creature.

Baby Blaze was a tiny little colt that had to struggle to survive from

the moment he came into this world.

  Blaze's Mother was very old when she had him and was really to old to have anymore colts. she belonged to a horrible old farmer that didn't take care of her or make sure she had enough to eat.

  It was very late in the year and was starting to get cold when the old mare had Baby Blaze.

  Blaze needed plenty of his Mother's milk to make him strong for those winter months ahead. She loved her little colt but she just wasn't able to provide enough milk for him without food for herself.

  Baby Blaze's Mother was able to feed him just enough to keep him alive, but without help from the cruel farmer winter was beginning to take

a toll on him. The lack of food and shelter from the cold had caused his legs to bend and twist.

Day after day the tiny colt would lay there in the pasture and then struggle to get up and drink what little milk he could get from his Mother.

Winter came that year with a terrible sting. Freezing rain and

snow covered the little horse's body as he slipped deeper into despair. The beautiful thick coat that had once covered him was now rotting away as the ice and snow blistered his skin.

People drove past that farm every day watching all hope slowly fade away from the tiny colt and yet no one stopped.

Baby Blaze knew he wouldn't survive to see the new grass of spring, but he told his Mother that night before he drifted off to sleep that he would keep trying. He never expected to see another day.

They were just a couple of little girls that lived down the road from the farm where Baby Blaze was living.

They knew nothing about farm life and certainly nothing about taking care of horses. They had been by the farm a few times and had seen the terrible condition the little colt was in.

Unlike everyone else that drove by they had their Father stop one day and ask the farmer about Blaze.

He told them he knew the colt wasn't doing good but he didn't want him and if they wanted to take him home they could have him.

So that day, the very day Blaze had given up all hope, the girls came and took him away from that horrible old farmer.

The two little girls and their Father had to get Baby Blaze up and then they helped him walk back to their house down the road. They didn't have a barn so they made a place for Blaze in their garage.

They spent the next few weeks feeding and caring for Baby Blaze. They had a doctor come out to give him medicine for the infection in his lungs. They gave him special baths for the sores on his skin.

Once the little colt started showing signs of improving they realized they needed to find him a permanent home. A nice farm with nice people to care for him. They would make sure he would never be unwanted and unloved again....

Ms. Charlene knows a lot of people that help rescue and find homes for unwanted animals around here.

One day she got a call from one of those friends asking if she knew of someone willing to give a little tiny colt a home.

The woman told Ms. Charlene about Baby Blaze and everything he had been through. She said two little girls had him living in their garage and needed to find him a good

forever home.

Ms. Charlene didn't have room for another horse at the time, but she thought of her dear friend Ms. Marie and knew she would be willing to take this little colt.

The next morning Ms. Charlene and Ms. Marie hooked up the horse trailer and headed down to the place where Baby Blaze had been living.

After praising the little girls for being brave enough to rescue this tiny colt they loaded him in the trailer and headed to his new home.

It has taken Ms. Marie a long time to undo the harm the cruel farmer did to Baby Blaze that winter, but each day he gets a little stronger and those old wounds of neglect are almost gone.

I don't think you could find anyone else that loves a little colt with twisted legs more than Ms. Marie does. She thinks he is the most beautiful horse in the pasture.

Baby Blaze has everything he could ever need here at Ms. Marie's. Lots of love and the new grass of spring for many springs to come.

Conclusion

You know it's funny how love can change the world. Nowadays I spend my time sitting on Ms. Charlene's front porch watching the lives that are changed by love and a second chance.

Ms. Charlene says what is important in this life is reaching out to the unwanted and unloved. Offering hope to the hopeless. Remembering those lost and forgotten.

She says every living creature was intended to have just that and as long as she is able she will spend her days doing what she can to help those who can't help themselves.

You know to others we may look like a bunch of mutts and ragamuffins, but to Ms. Charlene we are all purebreds. I know every single day here at the ranch that I am loved and wanted.

Oh the Black Dog Ranch isn't really a ranch. It's just a little bitty farm on an old dusty road way out in

the middle of nowhere, But it's home, it's my home.

Well I better go for now. I hear Ms. Charlene calling and that means it's suppertime around here.
I'm sure I'll have more stories to tell you another day. You never know who Ms. Charlene is going to bring home with her tomorrow.

Mia

About the Author

Kristie C. Jones has devoted most of her life to the rescue and rehabilitation of abandoned, abused and unwanted dogs and horses. She lives with Mia and the others on a small farm in Southeast Missouri.

    Her hope is that this book will encourage more people to adopt dogs like Mia that derserve a loving home and a second chance.